The Essence of

EASTER

The Essence of
EASTER

CRAIG A. CARDON

Covenant Communications, Inc.

Cover image *The Garden of the Empty Tomb* © Linda Curley Christensen, www.lindacurley.com

Cover design by Christina Marcano © 2022 by Covenant Communications, Inc.

Published by Covenant Communications, Inc.
American Fork, Utah

Printed in the United States of America
First Printing: February 2022

28 27 26 25 24 23 22   10 9 8 7 6 5 4 3 2 1

ISBN 978-1-52442-065-9

"He is not here: for he is risen."[1]

MILLENNIA AGO, ANGELS[2] UTTERED THESE words as the light of dawn broke upon that first Easter morning in Jerusalem. These angels brought hopeful wonder and growing joy to the hearts of the faithful women who had gathered at the empty sepulchre. And from that time forward, with this declaration, all of Christendom would rejoice in celebration of the most transcendent event in human history.

We recognize that the redeeming, enabling, and healing power of Jesus Christ afforded us by His Atonement can be applied daily, and that the universal applicability of His Resurrection brings consolation and peace, especially with the passing of a loved one. While we joyously participate in the annual celebration of the Savior's birth at Christmastime, it is at Easter time that we have the opportunity to more profoundly grasp the significance and meaning of the Savior's unique, inimitable role in our lives because of His Atonement and Resurrection.

In solemn affirmation of the Savior's role, the First Presidency and Council of the Twelve Apostles of The Church of Jesus Christ of Latter-day Saints made the following declaration in "The Restoration of the Fulness of the Gospel of Jesus Christ," their bicentennial proclamation to the world: "This Church is anchored in the perfect life of its chief cornerstone, Jesus Christ, and in His infinite Atonement and literal Resurrection."[3]

Through His Atonement and Resurrection, Jesus Christ did for all of our Heavenly Father's children what we could never do for ourselves: He not only overcame physical death and provided the means for overcoming spiritual death, but with all-encompassing compassion, "he [also took] upon him the pains and the sicknesses of his people," thereby "[knowing] according to the flesh how to succor his people according to their infirmities,"[4] and how to heal those who are "afflicted in any manner."[5] He suffered all this of His own volition, exercising His agency and willingly submitting His will to His Father's will. There was no compulsion—only love unfeigned. Charity. The pure love of Christ. The essence of Easter.

The Essence of Easter

During the time of our Savior's mortal ministry, there were those who were recognized as religious leaders of the Jewish faith, known as scribes, Pharisees, and elders, who were responsible for teaching the law of Moses and related religious practices. Over the centuries, an "oral tradition" of interpreting the law developed, and the Jewish leaders considered these spoken interpretations to be of equal value to the written law.[6] The leaders' adherence to the "tradition of the elders"[7] added unauthorized provisions to the law, and the spirit of the law had long since been lost to numerous prohibitions and uninspired practices. The law of Moses became obscured by secondary lists of dos and don'ts. Much like when we take unfiltered, trending information available today as complete truth rather than looking to reputable sources or our leaders, for the scribes and Pharisees, things of lesser consequence regularly took priority over things of much greater importance because of the prominence with which the lesser things were promoted through the persuasions and traditions of men.

Near the end of His mortal ministry, the Savior spoke to these religious leaders and severely chastised them for their errors and lack of understanding in teaching the people. Among His chastisements, He said, "Woe unto you, scribes and Pharisees, hypocrites! for ye pay tithe of mint and anise and cummin, and have omitted the weightier matters of the law, judgment, mercy, and faith: these ought ye to have done, and not to leave the other undone."[8] In focusing on the second things, such as a tithe on herbs, the scribes and Pharisees omitted the much more important first things of judgment, mercy, and faith.

The Savior made clear that while they should not ignore important things such as tithing, they should give first priority to foundational doctrine and principles.

There may be similar tendencies among some of us today. We sometimes become so focused on important, easy-to-measure, programmatic aspects of gospel living (second things) that we don't allow time for the essential, difficult-to-measure, heart-changing aspects of the gospel, the "weightier matters" (first things). Second things could include scripture reading, prayer, and church attendance, which, although necessary and important, are sometimes done simply to show outward compliance and not to experience any inner commitment or conversion. First things require recognizing and responding to the voice of the Spirit, in which there can be no duplicity. These first things are personal and require introspection.

When focusing on first and second things in the gospel, we may occasionally wish we could make clear distinctions between the two, but this is not always possible or wise. It is helpful, for example, to think about gospel doctrine, principles, and applications (or practices). There may be a clear distinction between the "doctrine" of the Godhead and the "practice" of something like saying amen at the end of a prayer. But there is important commonality and overlap between the "doctrine" of Christ and the first "principles" and "ordinances" [applications] of the gospel.[9] Nevertheless, as a general guide, first things tend to be on the doctrinal end of a doctrine-principle-application spectrum, while second things tend to be on the application end. Occasions also arise where the choice is simply between sustaining or opposing doctrine, principles, or applications rather than prioritizing them.

All gospel doctrine, principles, and applications are important, and many are essential. Their importance in individual lives may vary from time to time, depending on whether individual hearts are truly "converted" or are merely "compliant." Easter affords us a focused opportunity to more readily adhere to first things and move our hearts more fully to conversion.

Easter affords us a focused opportunity to more readily adhere to first things and move our hearts more fully to conversion.

Of the first things that must be our highest priority in living the gospel of Jesus Christ, foremost is having a testimony of Jesus Christ's Atonement, His Resurrection, and the place of His divine mission within our Father's plan.

For ancient Israel, God prescribed that they observe annual feasts in commemoration of the sacred events that had preserved His people while also foreshadowing the eventual advent of the Savior.[10] In our day, God has prescribed a weekly "feast"—the sacrament, an ordinance[11] in which His people individually partake of sacred emblems representing the body and blood of the Son of God in memory of His Atonement and

Resurrection. In partaking of the sacrament, do we merely comply, or are we deeply converted? Easter, the annual commemoration of the Savior's Atonement and Resurrection, affords us the opportunity as individuals, families, and believers to voluntarily and introspectively feast upon the words and deeds of Christ and to ponder their personal meaning more deeply.

Jacob taught, "For why not speak of the atonement of Christ, and attain to a perfect knowledge of him."[12] That perfect knowledge must be Spirit-borne, for no matter how exhaustively one studies Jesus Christ and His mission, "no man can say that Jesus is the Lord, but by the Holy Ghost."[13]

In learning about the life and mission of Jesus Christ by study and by faith,[14] we come to understand that His Atonement and Resurrection are not independent, isolated incidents of divine intervention occurring in the expanse of time. Rather, they are the essential, consummate core of the divine plan of our loving Heavenly Father. This plan makes possible all that we are and all that we hope to become as we experience the challenges and the successes and the heartaches and the joys of this life. In one chapter of scripture alone, Alma refers to God's plan as "the great plan of salvation," "the great plan of happiness," "the plan of redemption," and "the great plan of mercy."[15] These are all descriptions of the same plan, with Jesus Christ at the center.

Heavenly Father's plan is essential to understanding the Savior's infinite Atonement and literal Resurrection. It is only within this plan's context—the premortal existence, the Creation, the Fall of man, and the Atonement and Resurrection of Jesus Christ—that we can hope to obtain a perfect knowledge of what Christ did for us. Though our mortal minds may not be fully capable of comprehending how the Savior accomplished His mission, and Heavenly Father has not revealed every detail and aspect of His plan, He has revealed all that is necessary for His plan to be understood and operational, enabling us to choose to exercise faith in Jesus Christ and return to our Heavenly Father and be like Him.

More than a holiday celebration, then, this testimony of Jesus Christ, a first thing, becomes a personal, sacred quest—especially at Easter time—to gain knowledge of the assurance of resurrection and the hope of exaltation, as well as the blessing, even the promise, of healing,[16] peace,[17] and joy.[18]

As we consider the four parts of the plan, we will see how each relates to the great culminating events of Easter. The premortal existence, where Heavenly Father presented His plan and we all exercised faith in Jesus Christ. The Creation of the earth and of physical bodies for Adam and Eve, with the essential gift of agency preserved. The Fall, when Adam and Eve valiantly chose first things. The first Easter, the Atonement and Resurrection of Jesus Christ, thus doing for us what we could never do for ourselves. We will thereby be able to see ourselves more clearly within Heavenly Father's plan and more fully comprehend the meaning of Easter.

OUR PREMORTAL EXISTENCE

We know that we are spirit sons and daughters of heavenly parents.[19] We knew God, our Heavenly Father, during our premortal existence. We learned there, in council with Him, that He has a plan for us. Consider the significance of the name given to this premortal council in the scriptures: "the Council of the Eternal

God."[20] That council was so important that He gave it His own name, and we were a part of it! The scriptures provide additional important information about this premortal existence. We learn that "intelligences . . . were organized before the world was. . . . And God saw these souls that they were good, . . . for he stood among those that were spirits. . . . And he said unto those who were with him: We will go down, for there is space there, and we will take of these materials, and we will make an earth whereon these may dwell; And we will prove them herewith, to see if they will do all things whatsoever the Lord their God shall command them."[21]

Are you able to see yourself in this premortal existence? Can you imagine how you may have felt as the Father's plan was presented, including the need for a Savior, whereby you would have opportunity to become like the Father? Perhaps in our Easter quest for greater understanding and personalization of our Heavenly Father's plan, you will feel to join with Job as he spoke of "when the morning stars sang together, and all the sons of God shouted for joy."[22] Imagine how you felt in that premortal realm as we were given agency—the ability to think and to act independently. This ability included the capacity to understand and evaluate all we would experience in our premortal life and in this mortal life, which means we understood that there would be consequences for our thoughts and actions, both good and bad.[23]

Heavenly Father knew that inevitable negative consequences would forever estrange His children from His presence. His loving purpose, however, is "to bring to pass the immortality and eternal life of man."[24] To accomplish His purpose, He provided a Savior, the only means by which we, His spirit children, could have the hope of returning to His presence and of being like Him.

Our moral agency and our accountability were and are central to Heavenly Father's plan.[25] Simply stated, God's "prov[ing]"—or testing—us could not occur without our ability to make choices through the exercise of agency. For there to be choices, as Lehi states, there "must needs be . . . opposition." Otherwise, "all things must needs be a compound in one" with "no purpose."[26] It was Satan who opposed Heavenly Father's plan by seeking to negate agency and the need for a Savior.[27]

The Lord told Joseph Smith, "An angel of God who was in authority in the presence of God . . . rebelled against the Only Begotten Son . . . [and] was thrust down from the presence of God and the Son. . . . He was Lucifer, a son of the morning."[28]

The Lord told Moses, "Wherefore, because that Satan rebelled against me, and sought to destroy the agency of man . . . I caused that he should be cast down."[29]

John the Revelator explained, "There was war in heaven. . . . And the great dragon was cast out, that old serpent, called the Devil, and Satan. . . . And they overcame him by the blood of the Lamb, and by the word of their testimony."[30]

Because of Satan's opposition, our "prov[ing]" involves making choices centered on exercising faith in Jesus Christ. This faith-based means of choosing provides an important pattern in identifying and focusing on first things.

Exercising faith in Jesus Christ in the face of opposition did not begin with our earthly existence; our faith was fully active in the premortal existence, as evidenced by our willingness to follow God's plan to come to Earth. Heavenly Father explained, "They who keep their first estate," that is, exercise faith in Jesus Christ in the premortal existence by choosing to follow Him, "shall be added upon," meaning they will receive physical bodies on Earth; "and they who keep not their first estate" will not receive physical bodies. He continued to explain that "they who keep their second estate," meaning they receive physical bodies and again exercise faith in Jesus Christ during their mortal existence by following Him, will "have glory added upon their heads for ever and ever."[31]

With Heavenly Father's plan operative in both our premortal existence and our earthly existence, exercising agency was, now is, and always will be founded not just on exercising faith in general but on exercising faith in the Lord Jesus Christ. This is a core first thing.

The Savior and the agency of man are central to our Heavenly Father's plan. Heavenly Father made this known in the Council in Heaven[32] and has made it known in our mortal existence.[33] Our presence on Earth evidences that we, and all those around us, exercised faith in Him in our first estate, some even "exceedingly great faith,"[34] that the Savior would exercise His agency and choose to do the Father's will in all things. The question for all of us is, then, Will we exercise faith in this second estate?

Though we know the extreme importance of agency, we will do well to remember a word of caution about it: some may think—and may have encountered others who think—that the purpose of agency is to allow individuals the freedom to do whatever they want to do without facing negative consequences or accountability. While that limited understanding may be partially accurate in its own shallow realm, it obscures and diminishes the much deeper meaning. One of the core purposes of agency is to allow us the opportunity to choose to exercise faith in the Lord Jesus Christ. In doing so, we also choose to do the will of the Father.

Our Heavenly Father will never take away our agency. If there is any doubt about that, remember that He has already lost a third part[35] of His spirit children in preserving agency. Through the opposition we encountered as those spirits were lost in our premortal existence, we learned that giving priority to first things, beginning with faith in the Lord Jesus Christ, in our exercise of agency will bring us and those we love everlasting joy.

Our understanding of these things helps us connect them to Easter and better understand the need for the Creation of an earth and of physical bodies.

Exercising agency was, now is, and always will be founded not just on exercising faith in general but on exercising faith in the Lord Jesus Christ.

THE CREATION

According to the plan, the Gods "organized and formed the heavens and the earth."[36] We call this the Creation. We know that it was Jesus Christ in His premortal state who created all things under the direction of His Father.

The Book of Mormon prophet Samuel declared, "Jesus Christ . . . [is] the Father of heaven and of earth, the Creator of all things from the beginning."[37]

John the Beloved affirmed, "All things were made by him; and without him was not any thing made that was made."[38]

Moses explained that the Creation included the formation of physical bodies for Adam and Eve, which Heavenly Father personally created: "And I, God, said unto mine Only Begotten, which was with me from the beginning: Let us make man in our image, after our likeness; and it was so. . . . And I, God, created man in mine own image, in the image of mine Only Begotten created I him; male and female created I them."[39]

Abraham provides a few more specifics: "And the Gods formed man . . . and took his spirit (that is, the man's spirit), and put it into him; and breathed into his nostrils the breath of life, and man became a living soul. And the Gods planted a garden eastward in Eden, and there they put the man, whose spirit they had put into the body which they had formed."[40]

Moses adds, "And God blessed them, and God said unto them, Be fruitful, and multiply, and replenish the earth."[41]

As with our premortal existence, the Creation and the first commandment God gave to Adam and Eve to multiply and replenish the earth were essential elements in Adam and Eve's understanding of priorities and learning to act in faith on first things. Indeed, the opportunity for Heavenly Father's spirit sons and daughters to receive physical bodies on Earth is central to His eternal plan. Accordingly, we recognize that without the Creation of the earth and physical bodies, there would have been no possibility of mortal existence, and there would have been no Fall.

"And I, God, created man in mine own image, in the image of mine Only Begotten."

THE FALL OF MAN

Following the Creation, Adam and Eve were placed in the Garden of Eden in a paradisiacal state, meaning their bodies were not subject to physical death and they would have no children.[42] They were living souls with their spirit bodies and their physical bodies united, and they still possessed the precious gift of agency . . . always agency! As God told Enoch, "In the Garden of Eden, gave I unto man his agency."[43] It was in the garden that Adam and Eve experienced the Fall.

Although the particulars of Adam and Eve's experiences in the Garden of Eden are unique to them, in a representative sense, their story is the story of every son and daughter of God, because as a direct result of Adam's and Eve's choices, we all experience mortality. It is our story and an integral part of our Easter quest to comprehend and personalize first things.

In all that follows, consider how you would have felt and how you would have acted had you been in Adam and Eve's position.

Among all the lush vegetation of Eden, the Lord God "planted the tree of life . . . in the midst of the garden, and also the tree of knowledge of good and evil."[44] Having already given the first and higher commandment to Adam and Eve to multiply and replenish the earth, God now commanded them, saying, "Of every tree of the garden thou mayest freely eat, But of the tree of knowledge of good and evil, thou shalt not eat of it, nevertheless, thou mayest choose for thyself, for it is given unto thee; but, remember that I forbid it, for in the day thou eatest thereof thou shalt surely die."[45]

Because of the unique commandments and circumstances in the garden, the gift of agency was perfectly preserved. Indeed, the fact that Satan "beguiled our first parents"[46] affirms the reality of their agency; although they had been deceived in some things while in this state of innocence, they still knew all that God had commanded them. A central part of the "prov[ing]" in the garden was to see if Adam and Eve would recognize and choose to follow first things—the highest good embraced in the Father's plan. Such choices would provide the means for the Father's spirit children to receive physical bodies on Earth and the opportunity for them to exercise their agency in mortality. For Adam and Eve to make such a choice would necessitate their exercising faith in Jesus Christ as they did in the premortal existence.

Some may criticize the actions of Adam and Eve, but we honor them and gratefully acknowledge that they partook of the fruit of the tree of knowledge of good and evil, thus allowing our participation in our Father's plan: "Adam fell that men might be; and men are, that they might have joy."[47]

In addressing the Fall, latter-day scriptures and prophets describe Adam's and Eve's actions as a "transgression" rather than as a "sin." Lehi explains, "If Adam had not transgressed he would not have fallen," adding that Adam and Eve "would have remained in a state of innocence."[48]

Jacob states, "The fall came by reason of transgression."[49]

Moses records that the Lord Himself instructed Adam to teach his children freely, saying, "That by reason of transgression cometh the fall."[50]

President Joseph Fielding Smith explained the distinction between transgression and sin as follows:

> I never speak of the part Eve took in this fall as a sin, nor do I accuse Adam of a sin. One may say, "Well did they not break a commandment?" Yes. But let us examine the nature of that commandment and the results which came out of it.

> In no other commandment the Lord ever gave to man, did he say: . . . *"nevertheless, thou mayest choose for thyself"* [Moses 3:17]. . . .
>
> It is not always a sin to transgress a law. . . . [*Adam's*] *transgression was in accordance with law.* . . . This was a transgression of the law, but not a sin in the strict sense, for it was something that Adam and Eve had to do![51]

President Dallin H. Oaks, after quoting President Joseph Fielding Smith, taught the following:

> This suggested contrast between a *sin* and a *transgression* reminds us of the careful wording in the second article of faith: "We believe that men will be punished for their own *sins*, and not for Adam's *transgression*" (emphasis added). It also echoes a familiar distinction in the law. Some acts, like murder, are crimes because they are inherently wrong. Other acts, like operating without a license, are crimes only because they are legally prohibited. Under these distinctions, the act that produced the Fall was not a sin—inherently wrong—but a transgression—wrong because it was formally prohibited. These words are not always used to denote something different, but this distinction seems meaningful under the circumstances of the Fall.[52]

With this understanding, the testimonies of Adam and Eve, as Moses recorded, have great clarity. They acknowledge the importance of prioritizing first things and are testimonies that may also swell within our hearts.

> And in that day Adam blessed God and was filled, and began to prophesy concerning all the families of the earth, saying: Blessed be the name of God, for because of my transgression my eyes are opened, and in this life I shall have joy, and again in the flesh I shall see God.
>
> And Eve, his wife, heard all these things and was glad, saying: Were it not for our transgression we never should have had seed, and never should have known good and evil, and the joy of our redemption, and the eternal life which God giveth unto all the obedient.[53]

In a related thought, Mormon wrote to his son, Moroni, and said these words of Christ, "Little children are whole, for they are not capable of committing sin." And yet, little children sometimes do the wrong things. Perhaps in this light, when little children innocently disobey one of God's commandments, it may be said that they have transgressed the law. In any event, Mormon affirms, "Little children need no repentance, neither baptism. . . . But little children are alive in Christ."[54]

As part of His plan, God drove Adam and Eve, and by extension, us, out of the Garden of Eden and "placed at the east of the Garden of Eden, cherubim and a flaming sword, which turned every way to keep the way of the tree of life."[55] This lovingly ensured that they could not partake of the tree of life at that time and thereby live forever in their imperfect state.[56]

As Alma told his son, Corianton, "But behold, it was appointed unto man to die—therefore, as they were cut off from the tree of life they should be cut off from the face of the earth—and man became lost forever, yea, they became fallen man."[57]

By partaking of the forbidden fruit, Adam and Eve became subject to death, both physical and spiritual. Death is a separation. Physical death is the separation of the body and the spirit. Spiritual death is the separation of man from God's presence. By being cast out of the Garden of Eden, Adam and Eve experienced what the scriptures call a "first" spiritual death,[58] or separation from God. Their physical bodies changed from a paradisiacal state to a mortal state, meaning they were now subject to physical death. Because Adam and Eve had transgressed a commandment of God, they were now unclean and mortal. They could merit nothing of themselves.[59] Following their physical death, their spirits would never again be joined with their physical bodies,[60] and left to themselves, their spirits would forever be unclean and would, therefore, be unable to remain in the presence of God and dwell eternally with Him, for "no unclean thing can enter into his kingdom."[61] Thus, they would suffer what the scriptures call a "second" spiritual death.[62]

Men and women had, by nature, become "carnal, sensual, and devilish,"[63] "an enemy to God,"[64] in a "lost and fallen"[65] state. But, through the Atonement and Resurrection of Jesus Christ, there is hope—the hope we celebrate at Easter.

THE INFINITE ATONEMENT AND LITERAL RESURRECTION OF JESUS CHRIST

God is a "perfect, just God, and a merciful God also."[66] Both qualities—justice and mercy—are perfectly present in Him. Both are central to His plan. Both are central to the Atonement and Resurrection of the Lord Jesus Christ. In continuing to pursue our Easter quest to gain a deeper understanding of our Heavenly Father's divine plan, we will address God's perfect justice and His perfect mercy. In doing so, we will again consider Adam and Eve. In reviewing the account of Adam and Eve, we are reviewing our own story and our willingness to personally embrace the first things of the gospel, as Adam and Eve did.

God told Adam and Eve that if they partook of the forbidden fruit, they would die. Satan subsequently persuaded them to disobey God with a half-truth, saying, "Ye shall not surely die" (a lie), but rather, "ye shall be as gods, knowing good and evil" (a partial truth since the essential truth, "knowing good and evil," is only one part of being "as gods").[67]

Adam and Eve partook of the fruit and became subject to God's justice, with punishment to be imposed by what the scriptures call the "sword of justice."[68] God's justice is infinite and eternal. It is perfect.

Consider the way in which justice is regularly portrayed in human society. Often, the ideal of perfect justice is portrayed by a blindfolded female form holding balance scales in one hand and a sword in the other. The blindfold symbolizes that perfect justice is completely impartial. Perfect justice does not care if you are male or female or if you are rich or poor. Perfect justice does not care how young or old you are or if you are mentally or emotionally unaccountable. Perfect justice doesn't care what race you are. Justice doesn't even care if you are an infant. Perfect justice is completely blind, completely impartial.

The balance scales symbolize judgment, the means by which the actions of men are measured against the law.

The sword symbolizes the prescribed punishment that is administered once someone's actions are weighed against the law and found wanting.[69]

As God had forewarned, Adam and Eve's actions were weighed against His law, and Adam and Eve were found wanting. Now imagine that the sword of justice began to fall upon Adam and Eve, just as they deserved. With this punishment, their spirits would be separated from their bodies, never again to be united (no resurrection), and having been cast from the presence of God, they would never be worthy to reenter His presence (never overcoming the first or second spiritual death). Thus, their spirits would "become like unto [Satan] . . . angels to a devil."[70]

Imagine in that moment, the Savior stepping forward and positioning Himself, as Abinadi states,[71] between justice and Adam and Eve—between justice and you—and stopping justice's punishment from falling on them—and you.

Standing between justice and Adam and Eve, the Savior, in essence, turned to justice and said: *Justice, if you punish Adam and Eve now to satisfy your demands, they will never have the opportunity to become like Heavenly Father and be with Him eternally. They are imperfect and fallen and cannot merit anything of themselves.[72] They have no capacity to meet your perfect, infinite, and eternal demands for being exalted or receiving any other degree of glory, according to Heavenly Father's plan.*

However, if you will stay your punishment and allow a period of probation for them (and for all the Father's children),[73] I will come to Earth in the meridian of time[74] and voluntarily submit myself to the will of the Father on behalf of all His children.[75] Because I am perfect, infinite, and eternal, my atoning sacrifice will fully satisfy your perfect, infinite, and eternal demands required for the Father's children to inherit degrees of glory, according to their circumstances and their obedience to my gospel.[76] *And by all this, the Father will be glorified.*[77]

As for physical death, I have received from the Father power to lay down my life and power to take it up again.[78] *With my Resurrection, I will overcome physical death unconditionally for Adam and Eve and for all mankind. "The spirit and the body shall be reunited again in its perfect form . . . and [they] shall be brought to stand before God . . . and have a bright recollection of all [their] guilt."*[79]

As for spiritual death, "all, both old and young, both bond and free, both male and female, both the wicked and the righteous . . . shall be brought and be arraigned before the bar of Christ the Son, and God the Father, and the Holy Spirit . . . to be judged according to their works."[80]

Imagine the Savior continuing. *With everyone being brought before this bar, I will unconditionally overcome the first spiritual death, for all shall return to the presence of the Father,*[81] *even if temporarily.*

However, there is a second spiritual death resulting from men's transgressions and sins during mortality because "no unclean thing can enter into [the Father's] kingdom."[82] *For those who die before reaching the age of accountability and for those who are otherwise unaccountable before God,* [83] *I will unconditionally take upon me their transgressions, thereby overcoming the second spiritual death. For those who live to the age of accountability and beyond,*[84] *I will conditionally take upon me their sins, thereby overcoming the second spiritual death. The conditions are that they believe on my name and obey my gospel.*

For those who are valiant in their testimonies of me, according to their circumstances and diligence in obeying my gospel, my sacrifice will meet your demands in allowing them to be exalted and dwell eternally with the Father.[85] *For those*

Imagine the Savior then mercifully turning to Adam and Eve—and to us—and saying: I will do for you what you could never do for yourselves.

who are not valiant in their testimonies of me and who do not fully obey my gospel, my sacrifice will meet your demands in allowing them to inherit lesser degrees of glory, where even the least glory surpasses all understanding,[86] *but they will not live in the presence of the Father.*[87] *For those few who come to know me and are partakers of my power and then put me to shame, although they will be resurrected, there will be no forgiveness, and in accordance with your demands, they will not be redeemed, and they will receive no glory.*[88] *They will become the sons of perdition.*

With this supreme expression of mercy and in accordance with Heavenly Father's plan, justice was stayed and a period of probation was granted[89] and Adam and Eve began their mortal sojourn. This ensured that all our Father's spirit children who kept their first estate would enjoy the blessing of mortality.

Imagine the Savior then mercifully turning to Adam and Eve—and to us—and saying: *I will do for you what you could never do for yourselves. You have no capacity of yourselves to resurrect your bodies after physical death. I will come in the meridian of time, and I will overcome physical death for all. All will be resurrected.*

By my Resurrection, I will overcome not only physical death, but I will also redeem all men from the first spiritual death, because with their resurrection, all will be brought back into the presence of God to be judged.[90]

However, as imperfect, finite, fallen beings, you merit nothing of yourselves. You are wholly incapable of meeting the demands of justice for your sins, thereby overcoming the second spiritual death. But you can meet my requirements. My requirements are that you believe on my name and obey my gospel. My gospel is that you exercise faith in me, the Lord Jesus Christ, that you repent when you do wrong, that you are baptized and receive the gift of the Holy Ghost, and that you endure to the end, hearkening to my voice and the voice of my servants, obeying my commandments and ordinances.[91]

Imagine the Savior continuing: *Because I will "suffer temptations, and pain of body, hunger, thirst, and fatigue, even more than man can suffer,"*[92] *and be afflicted with all your afflictions,*[93] *according to your individual circumstances and the Father's will, I will take upon me your infirmities*[94] *as you face the challenges of mortality and exercise faith in me. I will give you power to do mighty things,*[95] *to withstand temptation,*[96] *to be delivered,*[97] *and I will heal those who are afflicted in any manner.*[98] *I will bear your griefs, and carry your sorrows.*[99] *I will give you peace.*[100] *I will redeem you, enable you, and heal you.*

"Yea, come unto [me], and be perfected in [me] . . . then is [my] grace sufficient for you. . . . And again, if ye by the grace of God are perfect in [me] and deny not [my] power, then are ye sanctified in [me] by the grace of God, through the shedding of [my blood], which is in the covenant of the Father unto the remission of your sins, that ye become holy, without spot."[101]

With faith in Jesus Christ, Adam and Eve agreed, and thus, our Father's plan of happiness became available to

---

"Yea, come unto [me], and be perfected in me . . . then is [my] grace sufficient for you."

---

them and to all of us. Even those who would die physically without having the opportunity to receive the gospel of Jesus Christ and exercise faith in Him in this life would have that opportunity in the next life, in the spirit world, before the final judgment.[102] As the prophets have taught, "All mankind were in a lost and in a fallen state, and ever would be save they should rely on this Redeemer."[103] Our reliance on the Savior is not in vain. As promised, Jesus Christ came in the meridian of time to atone for the sins of the world.

While contemplating the Savior's Atonement, many have attempted to describe what He experienced during His final visit to the Garden of Gethsemane. Perhaps each of us would benefit from such an attempt. Though there is frequent acknowledgment that words are insufficient to describe what we know occurred in the garden, we read in the inspired words of Elder James E. Talmage:

> Christ's agony in the garden is unfathomable by the finite mind, both as to intensity and cause. The thought that He suffered through fear of death is untenable. Death to Him was preliminary to resurrection and triumphal return to the Father from whom He had come, and to a state of glory even beyond what He had before possessed; and, moreover, it was within His power to lay down His life voluntarily. He struggled and groaned under a burden such as no other being who has lived on Earth might even conceive as possible. It was not physical pain, nor mental anguish alone, that caused Him to suffer such torture as to

produce an extrusion of blood from every pore; but a spiritual agony of soul such as only God was capable of experiencing. No other man, however great his powers of physical or mental endurance, could have suffered so; for his human organism would have succumbed, and syncope would have produced unconsciousness and welcome oblivion. In that hour of anguish Christ met and overcame all the horrors that Satan, "the prince of this world" could inflict. The frightful struggle incident to the temptations immediately following the Lord's baptism was surpassed and overshadowed by this supreme contest with the powers of evil.

In some manner, actual and terribly real though to man incomprehensible, the Savior took upon Himself the burden of the sins of mankind from Adam to the end of the world. Modern revelation assists us to a partial understanding of the awful experience. In March 1830, the glorified Lord, Jesus Christ, thus spake: "For behold, I, God, have suffered these things for all, that they might not suffer if they would repent, but if they would not repent, they must suffer even as I, which suffering caused myself, even God, the greatest of all, to tremble because of pain, and to bleed at every pore, and to suffer both body and spirit: and would that I might not drink the bitter cup and shrink—nevertheless, glory

be to the Father, and I partook and finished
my preparations unto the children of men"
(Doctrine and Covenants 19:16–19).[104]

Elder Talmage shared the following companion per-
spective of the Crucifixion at Golgotha:

> It seems, that in addition to the fearful suf-
> fering incident to the crucifixion, the agony
> of Gethsemane had recurred, intensified
> beyond human power to endure. In that
> bitterest hour the dying Christ was alone,
> alone in the most terrible reality. That the
> supreme sacrifice of the Son might be
> consummated in all its fulness, the Fa-
> ther seems to have withdrawn the sup-
> port of His immediate Presence, leaving
> to the Savior of men the glory of complete
> victory over the forces of sin and death. . . .
>
> The period of faintness, the concep-
> tion of utter forsakenness soon passed,
> and the natural cravings of the body re-
> asserted themselves. . . .
>
> Fully realizing that He was no longer
> forsaken, but that His atoning sacrifice
> had been accepted by the Father, and that
> His mission in the flesh had been carried
> to glorious consummation, He exclaimed
> in a loud voice of holy triumph: "*It is
> finished.*" In reverence, resignation, and
> relief, He addressed the Father saying:
> "*Father, into thy hands I commend my
> spirit.*" He bowed His head, and volun-
> tarily gave up His life.[105]

The Savior was crucified and gave up His life on the Friday of Passover. His body was hurriedly placed in the garden tomb before the setting of the sun. Three days later, according to the timing of the Jews, on the first day of the week, Sunday, "when it was yet dark,"[106] women went to the sepulchre, and "as it began to dawn,"[107] they heard the words of the angels, "He is risen."[108]

In marvelous affirmation of His divinity and in powerful testimony of the Atonement He had wrought, the scriptures record that in the following hours, days, and weeks, the Savior revealed His resurrected body to individuals, small groups, and large gatherings on at least ten occasions. The Resurrection itself is our Savior's witness to the world that He did the will of the Father and overcame physical and spiritual death. The following summary identifies those to whom he appeared:

Sunday morning—Easter

- Mary Magdalene (John 20:16; Mark 16:9).
- Women: Mary the mother of James, Salome, Joanna, the women (Matthew 28:1, 9; Mark 16:1; Luke 23:55; Luke 24:10).

Sometime on Sunday

- Peter/Cephas (Luke 24:34; 1 Corinthians 15:5).
- Cleopas and his companion—possibly Luke (Luke 24:31).

Sunday evening

- Ten Apostles and others (Luke 24:33, 36; John 20:19).

Sunday—one week later

- Eleven Apostles (John 20:26).

At the sea of Tiberias

* Seven Apostles (John 21:2, 7).

A mountain in Galilee

* Eleven Apostles and over five hundred brethren (Matthew 28:16–17; 1 Corinthians 15:6). These may have been two separate appearances.

Another occasion

* James, the Lord's brother, and all of the Apostles (1 Corinthians 15:7; Galatians 1:19). These may have been two separate appearances.

The day of ascension—after forty days of "showing himself alive after his passion by many infallible proofs" (Acts 1:3)

* The Apostles and others (Acts 1:10).

We are indebted to Adam and Eve for their role in effectuating the Father's plan. More than indebted to Christ, however, we are completely dependent on Him and His infinite Atonement and literal Resurrection, which provide the sole means by which the designs of the Father's plan are fully realized. What a blessing it is when the anniversary of these events comes before us and we again have opportunity to celebrate more purposefully the reality of their effect in our personal lives! Blessed Easter!

These events constitute the infinite Atonement and literal Resurrection of Jesus Christ, a first thing made known in our premortal existence that was foreshadowed for so long in this life by prescribed feasts and prophesied of since the Fall of man. But will we recognize it in our hearts? Will it move from outward performances or celebrations to an inward, personal, heart-changing acceptance of an eternal, essential gift so freely given? Will our hearts understand, accept, and act?

CONTEXT FOR SHARING

As we contemplate the personal implications of these eternal truths and study them individually, within our families, and among our friends, we see that when the prophets teach of the Atonement and Resurrection of Jesus Christ, they often do so within the context of the Father's plan, giving special attention to the Creation and the Fall.

The Lord Himself exemplified this in the book of Moses, providing a beautiful pattern as He taught Adam and then instructed Adam to teach his children of the Fall, of the need to repent, and of Jesus Christ.[109] The Lord concluded His teaching with these words: "This is the plan of salvation unto all men, through the blood of mine Only Begotten, who shall come in the meridian of time."[110]

Jacob's masterful sermon on the Atonement of Jesus Christ, as recorded in 2 Nephi 9, begins with this meaningful contextual declaration: "For as death hath passed upon all

---

"This is the plan of salvation unto all men, through the blood of mine Only Begotten."

---

men, to fulfil the merciful plan of the great Creator, there must needs be a power of resurrection, and the resurrection must needs come unto man by reason of the fall; and the fall came by reason of transgression; and because man became fallen they were cut off from the presence of the Lord."[111]

When Aaron went to the home of the king of the Lamanites (the father of king Lamoni), Aaron learned that the king knew very little about God and, therefore, knew virtually nothing about God's plan. From the scriptures, Aaron taught the king the plan of redemption through Christ, beginning with the Creation and the Fall: "And Aaron did expound unto him the scriptures from the creation of Adam, laying the fall of man before him, and their carnal state and also the plan of redemption, which was prepared from the foundation of the world, through Christ, for all whosoever would believe on his name."[112]

Alma the Younger had a son, Corianton, who temporarily went astray. Alma's teachings to this son comprise four chapters in the Book of Mormon, Alma 39–42. Alma taught Corianton about the Atonement and Resurrection of Jesus Christ within the context of our Father's plan, speaking of the Fall and of God's justice and mercy: "And thus we see that all mankind were fallen, and they were in the grasp of justice; yea the justice of God, which consigned them forever to be cut off from his presence. And now, the plan of mercy could not be brought about except an atonement should be made."[113]

These are helpful patterns to follow when sharing the fruits of our Easter quest. As the Apostle John recorded, "For God so loved the world, that he gave his only begotten Son, that whosoever believeth in him should not perish, but have everlasting life."[114]

CONCLUSION

So, what is the message of Easter? The angels declared it: He is risen! And when the angels made this declaration, they added a deeply meaningful invitation: "Come, see the place where the Lord lay."[115] Perhaps we individually can hear in this appeal not only an angelic invitation to see the emptiness of the tomb but also a divinely inspired invitation to see the suffering of Gethsemane and the agony of Golgotha and to see in all three places the redeeming elements of the Savior's faithful, voluntary fulfillment of His premortal commitment, "Here am I, send me."[116] Come, see the infinite Atonement and the literal Resurrection of the Lord Jesus Christ and see their central place in the Father's plan for you.

When the Savior appeared to His disciples on that first Easter, He wanted them to understand so they could declare to the world that by His literal Resurrection, He had conquered physical death for all: "Handle me, and see; for a spirit hath not flesh and bones, as ye see me have."[117] Beyond that physical witness, the Savior's literal Resurrection powerfully and conclusively affirms that He is the Son of God the Father and that, by virtue of the infinite Atonement, He has conquered spiritual death for those who believe on His name, obey His gospel, and endure to the end. Even now, He lovingly and graciously suffers "the pains of every living creature, both men, women, and children,"[118] bears their grief, and carries their sorrows,[119] accomplishing the will of the Father.

Consider the significance of four exemplary scriptures that, hopefully, will now have deeper meaning, borne from greater contextual understanding.

- And the days of the children of men were prolonged, according to the will of God, that they might repent while in the flesh; wherefore, their state became a state of probation.[120]

- Little children are redeemed from the foundation of the world through mine Only Begotten.[121]

- [The Son of God] having ascended into heaven, having the bowels of mercy; being filled with compassion towards the children of men; *standing betwixt them and justice;* having broken the bands of death, taken upon himself their iniquity and their transgressions, having redeemed them, and satisfied the demands of justice.[122]

- God himself atoneth for the sins of the world, to bring about the plan of mercy, to appease the demands of justice, that God might be a perfect, just God, and a merciful God also.[123]

When we understand the infinite Atonement and literal Resurrection of Jesus Christ, there are two phrases in the Book of Mormon that we will more readily comprehend. The phrases, similar to one another, are: "It must be an infinite atonement" and "It must be an infinite and eternal sacrifice."

In the first phrase, Jacob teaches the people of Nephi: "The fall came by reason of transgression; and because man became fallen they were cut off from the presence of the Lord. Wherefore, *it must needs be an infinite atonement.*"[124]

In the second phrase, Amulek teaches the Zoramites: "For it is expedient that there should be a great and last sacrifice; yea, not a sacrifice of man, neither of beast, neither of any manner of fowl; for it shall not be a human sacrifice; but *it must be an infinite and eternal sacrifice.*"[125]

The simple question is, Why? Why must there be an infinite and eternal sacrifice? One answer, that it is because God's creations are infinite and eternal in number and the Savior's Atonement is for all of them, provides a partial understanding. It is true that God's creations are infinite in number, and it is true that the Savior's Atonement is effective for all of them, but this does not fully grasp the deeper meaning.

It must be an infinite Atonement—an infinite and eternal sacrifice—because only an infinite and eternal atonement or sacrifice can meet the demands of God's infinite and eternal justice. It is that simple, and it is that profound!

Understanding and personalizing the infinite Atonement and literal Resurrection of Jesus Christ are the essence of Easter and the focus of our Easter quest. They are the very first things in the foundational doctrine of the gospel of Jesus Christ. There are other important, even essential, second things, but throughout our earthly existence, if we will personally be converted to these first things and do all we can to share them with others, and if we will share second things, always within the context of these first things, the Lord will bless us and magnify our efforts.

We cannot understand the need to meet the demands of God's perfect justice unless we understand the Fall of man. And we cannot understand the Fall of man unless we understand the Creation. And we cannot understand the Creation unless we understand our premortal existence and God's plan presented there, the plan of mercy.

With understanding, one may powerfully declare to all the world that Jesus Christ is the only name under heaven whereby man may be saved.

However, with understanding, one may powerfully declare to all the world that Jesus Christ is the only name under heaven whereby man may be saved. As Lehi so boldly proclaimed: "Wherefore, redemption cometh in and through the Holy Messiah; for he is full of grace and truth. Behold, he offereth himself a sacrifice for sin, to answer the ends of the law, unto all those who have a broken heart and a contrite spirit; and unto none else can the ends of the law be answered. Wherefore, how great the importance to make these things known unto the inhabitants of the earth, that they may know that there is no flesh that can dwell in the presence of God, save it be through the merits, and mercy, and grace of the Holy Messiah."[126]

Jesus Christ is the Savior of the World. He met the demands of justice for all of us, and His is the only name under heaven by which we have hope of living eternally in the presence of God and being like Him. May this testimony and all the blessings of our Easter quest forever reside in our hearts and in the hearts of those we love.

ENDNOTES

1. Matthew 28:6.
2. JST Matthew 28:2; JST Mark 16:3; Luke 24:4.
3. The First Presidency and Council of the Twelve Apostles of The Church of Jesus Christ of Latter-day Saints, "The Restoration of the Fulness of the Gospel of Jesus Christ: A Bicentennial Proclamation to the World," General Conference, April 5, 2020.
4. Alma 7:11–12.
5. 3 Nephi 17:9.
6. Bible Dictionary, "Elders," "Pharisees," "Scribe."
7. Matthew 15:2; Mark 7:3.
8. Matthew 23:23.
9. The Articles of Faith 1:1–4.
10. Bible Dictionary, "Feasts."
11. JST Mark 14:20–26.
12. Jacob 4:12.
13. 1 Corinthians 12:3. While meeting with members of the "Female Relief Society" on April 28, 1842, the Prophet Joseph Smith said that this verse should be translated, "No man

can *know* that Jesus is the Lord, but by the Holy Ghost" (*History of the Church*, 4:602–603).

14. Doctrine and Covenants 88:118.

15. Alma 42:5, 8, 11, 15, 16, 31. (See also Alma 34:9, "plan of the Eternal God").

16. 3 Nephi 17:7; Doctrine and Covenants 112:13.

17. John 14:27; 16:33; Mark 4:39; 2 Nephi 19:6 (Isaiah 9:6); Doctrine and Covenants 59:23.

18. John 15:11; 16:20–24; 17:13; 2 Nephi 2:25; 8:3; 3 Nephi 12:11–12; Doctrine and Covenants 11:13.

19. "The Family: A Proclamation to the World," 1995.

20. Doctrine and Covenants 121:32.

21. Abraham 3:22–25.

22. Job 38:7.

23. Doctrine and Covenants 29:36; 93:29–32; Moses 4:3.

24. Moses 1:39.

25. Doctrine and Covenants 101:78.

26. 2 Nephi 2:11–12.

27. Moses 4:1–4; Abraham 3:27–28.

28. Doctrine and Covenants 76:25–26.

29. Moses 4:3.

30. Revelation 12:7–11.

31. Abraham 3:25–26.

32. Doctrine and Covenants 29:36; Abraham 3:27–28.

33. Mosiah 3:5–13.

34. Alma 13:3.

35. Revelation 12:4; Doctrine and Covenants 29:36.

36. Abraham 4:1.

37. Helaman 14:12.

38. John 1:3.

39. Moses 2:26–27. Also: "When it came to placing man on earth, there was a change in Creators. That is, the Father himself became personally involved. All things were created by the Son, using the power delegated by the Father, except man. In the spirit and again in the flesh, man was created by the Father. There was no delegation of authority where the crowning creature of creation was concerned" (Bruce R. McConkie, *The Promised Messiah: The First Coming of Christ* [Salt Lake City: Deseret Book Company, 1978], 62).
40. Abraham 5:7–8; see also Genesis 2:7–8; Moses 3:7–8.
41. Genesis 1:28.
42. 2 Nephi 2:22–23.
43. Moses 7:32; see also Doctrine and Covenants 29:35.
44. Moses 3:9.
45. Moses 3:16–17.
46. 2 Nephi 9:9; Mosiah 16:3; Ether 8:25.
47. 2 Nephi 2:25.
48. 2 Nephi 2:22–23.
49. 2 Nephi 9:6.
50. Moses 6:59.
51. Joseph Fielding Smith, *Doctrines of Salvation*, comp. Bruce R. McConkie, 3 vols. (Salt Lake City: Bookcraft, 1954–56), 1:114–115; emphasis in the original.
52. Dallin H. Oaks, "The Great Plan of Happiness," *Ensign*, November 1993.
53. Moses 5:10–11.
54. Moroni 8:8, 11–12.

55. Moses 4:31.

56. Alma 12:21, 26 (21–27); 42:3–4.

57. Alma 42:6.

58. Helaman 14:16.

59. Alma 22:14.

60. 2 Nephi 9:8–9.

61. 3 Nephi 27:19; 1 Nephi 10:21; Alma 11:37; Moses 6:57.

62. Helaman 14:18; Alma 12:16.

63. Mosiah 16:3; Alma 42:10; Doctrine and Covenants 20:20; Moses 5:13.

64. Mosiah 3:19.

65. Mosiah 16:4; Alma 12:22.

66. Alma 42:15.

67. Moses 4:10–11.

68. Helaman 13:5; 3 Nephi 20:20.

69. Daniel 5:27.

70. 2 Nephi 9:9.

71. Mosiah 15:9.

72. Alma 22:14.

73. Alma 12:24; 34:32–35; Doctrine and Covenants 29:42–43; 2 Nephi 2:21.

74. Moses 5:57; 6:57.

75. John 6:38; 3 Nephi 27:13.

76. Doctrine and Covenants 76:39–44.

77. Doctrine and Covenants 45:3–5; 132:63.

78. John 10:17–18.

79. Alma 11:43.

80. Alma 11:44.

81. Helaman 14:15–17; Alma 11:41–44.

82. 3 Nephi 27:19; 1 Nephi 10:21; Alma 11:37; 40:26.

83. Doctrine and Covenants 29:46–47; 74:7; Alma 29:5; Mosiah 3:16; 15:25; Moroni 8:8.

84. Moroni 8:10.

85. Doctrine and Covenants 76:50–70.

86. Doctrine and Covenants 76:89.

87. Doctrine and Covenants 76:71–90.

88. Doctrine and Covenants 76:31–38.

89. 1 Nephi 10:21; 2 Nephi 2:21; 9:27; Alma 34:32–
35; Helaman 13:38.

90. Helaman 14:15–17; Alma 11:41–44.

91. 2 Nephi 31:2–21; 3 Nephi 11:23–41; 27:13–29;
Ether 4:17–19; Doctrine and Covenants
124:45–6.

92. Mosiah 3:7.

93. Doctrine and Covenants 133:53.

94. Alma 7:11–12.

95. Jacob 4:7.

96. Alma 37:33.

97. Alma 14:26.

98. 3 Nephi 17:7–9.

99. Mosiah 14:3–5; Isaiah 53:3–5.

100. John 14:27.

101. Moroni 10:33–34.

102. Alma 40; Doctrine and Covenants 127, 128,
138.

103. 1 Nephi 10:6; see also Jacob 7:11–12; Mosiah
16:4.

104. James E. Talmage, *Jesus the Christ*, Deseret
Press, (Salt Lake City, 1915, 1916, 1973),
613–614.

105. James E. Talmage, *Jesus the Christ*, Deseret
Press, (Salt Lake City, 1915, 1916, 1973),
661–662.

106. John 20:1.

107. Matthew 28:1.

108. Matthew 28:6.

109. Moses 6:55–62.
110. Moses 6:62.
111. 2 Nephi 9:6; see all of 2 Nephi 9.
112. Alma 22:13 (1, 7–18).
113. Alma 42:14–15.
114. John 3:16.
115. Matthew 28:6.
116. Abraham 3:27.
117. Luke 24:39.
118. 2 Nephi 9:21.
119. Mosiah 14:4; Isaiah 53:4.
120. 2 Nephi 2:21; see also Alma 12:24; 42:4–6.
121. Doctrine and Covenants 29:46; see also Mosiah 3:16; 15:25; Alma 29:5; Moroni 8:12; Doctrine and Covenants 74:7.
122. Mosiah 15:9; emphasis added.
123. Alma 42:15; see also Alma 34:15–16; 42:22–26.
124. 2 Nephi 9:6–7; emphasis added.
125. Alma 34:10; emphasis added.
126. 2 Nephi 2:6–8.

ABOUT THE AUTHOR

CRAIG ALLEN CARDON WAS SUSTAINED as a General Authority Seventy of The Church of Jesus Christ of Latter-day Saints in 2006. He served as a member of the Africa West Area presidency, an assistant executive director in the Priesthood and Family Department, the editor of Church magazines, and a member of the Pacific Area presidency. He became an Emeritus General Authority in 2018.

He chaired committees in the Priesthood and Family Department that, under the direction of the Twelve Apostles, developed the new Come, Follow Me Church curriculum and the new children and youth initiatives.

He received an accounting degree from Arizona State University and a master of public administration degree from the Harvard Kennedy School with a methodological area of concentration in leadership and was named a Littauer Fellow. Prior to his General Authority calling in 2006, he was an entrepreneur with multiple business interests.

He is married to Deborah L. Dana, and they are the parents of eight children. As of the end of 2021, they have forty-six grandchildren and five great-grandchildren.